THE STRIPP

Michael O'Neill was born in
up in Liverpool. He read English at
Oxford, went on to complete a D.Ph
a lecturer in English at the University
1979. He co-founded and is an editor o.
a leading poetry magazine, and is a well-known
reviewer of contemporary poetry. He received an Eric
Gregory Award in 1983, and a selection of his poems
appeared in *The Gregory Poems 1983–84*. He is the
author of a critical study of Shelley's poetry, *The
Human Mind's Imaginings*, and also of *Percy Bysshe
Shelley: A Literary Life*. He is married with one child.

Michael O'Neill

THE STRIPPED BED

COLLINS HARVILL
8 Grafton Street, London W1
1990

Collins Harvill
William Collins Sons and Co Ltd
London · Glasgow · Sydney · Auckland
Toronto · Johannesburg

BRITISH LIBRARY CATALOGUING IN PUBLICATION DATA

O'Neill, Michael 1953–
The stripped bed
I. Title
821'.014

ISBN 0–00–271019–6

First published in Great Britain by Collins Harvill 1990
© Michael O'Neill 1990

Photoset in Monophoto Bembo by
Butler & Tanner Ltd, Frome and London
Printed and bound in Great Britain by
Hartnolls Limited, Bodmin, Cornwall

FOR POSY AND DANIEL

ACKNOWLEDGEMENTS

Acknowledgements are due to the editors of the following publications in which many of these poems (or versions of them) first appeared: *Critical Quarterly, Encounter, Listener, Literary Review, London Magazine, New Statesman, Outposts Poetry Quarterly, Oxford Poetry, Poetry Ireland Review, Poetry Review, Proceedings of the English Association North, Spectator, Sunday Times, Times Literary Supplement.*

Two poems appeared in *New Poetry 8* (Hutchinson in association with the Arts Council and PEN, 1982).

A collection including nine of these poems received an Eric Gregory Award in 1983, and seven poems appeared in *The Gregory Poems 1983–84* (The Salamander Press, 1985).

'The Last Visit' (originally printed in the *New Statesman*) appeared in *Beyond the Shore: The Irish Within Us* (Northampton Connolly Association, 1985).

CONTENTS

I

II

III

IV

I

The Neighbourhood

We moved up to "The Park", to a larger house.
Schoolfriends envied the attics.

At birthday parties, clattering like goats,
they'd leave me sheepishly behind, count stairs
– 23, 24, 25 – until they got their view:

beyond the walled-in gardens, iron-railed "Prom",
and serenaded by the gulls,
the Mersey washing our marginal world.

In dreams the sandbank sucked me slowly down.

A bulldozed plot squared up to us for months.
Gangs carved initials through heart-broken bark
– visiting-cards from a city we'd cut dead.

Our siege mentality. Two moons rose at night:
one for the bristling docks, one for my window.

Twopence to Cross the Mersey

She, too, moved to Liverpool as a child,
was the eldest of seven and when she spoke

sounded as though she had "ollies in her mouth".
There, our lives' resemblances end.

If she had caught a tram to our suburb,
she would have gasped to see how lushly

the grass grew on the fence's other side
just a few miles away from starving slums.

Wouldn't I have hurried past had I glimpsed
in once plush Bold Street what scared her so much:

a very thin thing . . . a wraithlike grey face
– her apparition in a dress-shop window? . . .

Taking the ferry she couldn't afford,
I'm midpoint, now, between two shores. Waves churn.

Father and Son

Your latest gadget – a "monocular" . . .
You showed it to me on our homeward walk

beside the Mersey, past that stuck-up sign,
This Park is Private – then used it

to spot birds ("more now the river's cleaner"):
"plovers and, look, they're dunlins by the tide."

I looked and joked – "Your fault my vision's poor" –
but swung round to the cranes at Garston Docks

as though the city would reveal itself.
"Each to his own picture." Perhaps I meant:

Don't you see what we share – your legacy –
this sense of belonging nowhere?

Engrossed by detail, lens in hand,
you unriddled the name on a ship's bow.

Back Home: the Boiler Room

The new boiler croons contentedly,
dialled interloper no one likes.
Its oil-gorged forebear growled through talks
at midnight, part of the family.

But now my childhood might be dust
beneath dynastic bikes, bust chairs.
Slowly an aura disappears.
Chipped tiles image the fracturing past.

I can still see my mother kneeling,
scrubbing this floor when we first came.
Compute the years: we are their sum.
The boiler sings, recalling nothing.

Exiles

Dispersed for months now – one to Italy,
one to the States . . . Yet that November night

– it holds you still, an island in the flow.

Had the Roscoe Arms ever heard the like?
"Scouse Punks" eavesdropped. The juke-box shushed.

Not that the volume, turned up, worried you.
"It's good, this track." The other bowed assent.

Nous, war veterans in Yugoslavia . . .
on you gassed. Smoke floated over my head.

Ladders of talk. Where did they lead? "The Forms . . ."

Ash flicked into beer. Pause. "Improves the flavour."
The pair of you put matter in its place,

mapped stars for me from icy Renshaw Street,
the white blooms of your breath coming and going.

Outside

Our Liverpool Catholic background?
We boast it like a badge, but
don't share the nasal twang which warms
this pub to life. Just open your mouth
and it's there, the spirit of a city.

You're a conjuror. I'm spellbound,
whisked back years to coffee bars,
bistros – wherever you chance on,
I seem to be watching rings of smoke
coolly lassoing tranced moments

while faces moon round tables . . .
And I still sit apart like a spy
whose cover's blown, fixated on a desk
where a boy gets by heart his latest
lesson: "you don't speak like us."

Serving

We'd kneel in a pew, totting up "mistakes" –
cruets bungled, bells that failed to ring . . .

We go back years; we served High Mass together,
comrades in cassocks, you an acolyte,
wax never trembling from your steadied candle.

A prima donna, I was thurifer,
idled, between turns, in the sacristy,
tempted by amber tints of altar wine.

Those grand entrances. While the priest swished on,
I'd bow to the people, then chink the chain
– right, left, ahead – until my incense bloomed.

What was it, though, that wilted? Requiems
meant silver hand-outs after we'd betrayed
no feeling for those graveside faces.

Speaking Terms

Deadpan, his fellow-Scousers dubbed him Einstein.
A hint of more than the thickness of glasses?
They glinted stonily when we played soccer.

We'd not swapped a word. One day in the yard
he solved the riddle of my fancy accent
with "you prat" – then stalked off, chuffed as a boffin.

Hardly an ice-breaker. Soon kickabouts
were just a pretext, class warfare the goal.
The upshot? Me riding a last-ditch tackle,
yet done for by the whiplash of his neck,

a butt intent on ramming home some point
he must have felt strongly. It's left
less of a mark than the vision of eyes
dilating with hate: our common language.

Lights, Lights!

The bridegroom crosses the marquee.
After he's fiddled with the dimmer-switch

the disco shifts into another gear.
Exhorted by the band's lead singer,

the younger guests start "to really get down".
I'm wedged behind a table with a drink,

back at that annual tussle, the school dance . . .
To turn the lights off was against the rule

it seemed a matter of honour to break
while the Boss patrolled tennis-courts, torch in hand.

A crazed voyeur? Stationed outside the Hall,
I shared the joke with other prefects, feigned

indifference to the pulse of sex
– as I do now, heading towards night air.

Facing the Music

I slip away while talk chinks
like long drinks laid down on glass tables.
Our hostess is tapping her first cigar.
Mulled shadows gatecrash coyly.

This bathroom's marbled gaudiness
will do as a refuge. I gawp
at the mirror. "Who are you?" query
wine-dilated eyes that seem another's.

Going back, I halt on a stair,
fingertips flexed against the wall,
steadying myself to face the music
of laughter vexing like sunlight through blinds.

Recreation

Our frisbee wavers on its yellow course
from hand to hand across the park. I think
"How solitary we are," and now trees drink
blackness from a winter sky, that bone-dry source.

Wanting to call the silence numinous,
I merely watch a vapour trail upset
the still sky like a creepy-crawly comet:
beneath it, lights in buildings spy on us.

Who are we in this hour of recreation?
All shapes are gathered by the darkening sky
save violet light, while, uttering its soft cry,
the frisbee dips towards my isolation.

Handwriting

"Strange," you murmur with a smile of insight
while deciphering ego-ridden loops
that throng the margins of my student Auden.
So much hot air buoyed up those inked balloons!

Do you glimpse what I must have been? Do I?
As if a trapdoor opened, I'm plunged back
between stark walls I know. A gas fire whistles
through solipsistic teeth. A young man turns

page after page with tense, devouring fury.
He's too absorbed to notice when I leave.
Just one more tenant occupying the room

of my life? When you say, "I think I like
your hard-to-read, collapsed script better," I smile
and stare towards identity's abyss.

The Irish Connection

"With your name you should plug the Irish connection,"
says a friend, his ear to the publishing ground

rather than my RP. "So near and yet ...!"
My uncle wrote *A History of the O'Neills*

in San Francisco; at school in Liverpool
roll call seemed to stick when the Brother reached O:

"O'Brien? O'Connor? O'Hara? O'Hare? ..."
A close friend from the same form learned Gaelic,

joined the Irish Foreign Office and married
a girl of Swedish descent in New York ...

It feels as though I'd missed a bus that chose
from some whim to take a parallel street

instead of mine, then moved off between houses,
a rumour of green at the edge of the eye.

Airfix

Monopoly, Totopoly – and on the floor
of the inset wardrobe, after that last nosedive,

a plastic tangle of wing, fuselage,
transfer and turret . . . An era had ended.

Kits cost half a crown and took a fortnight
to save up for; then the raid on Woolworths.

We came off clutching our spoils, our bagsed
mementoes of a war that seemed antique,

though less remote in years than we are now
from thrilled selves circa '63.

But you've the same frown when you concentrate.
I'm still the apprentice maker who botched

Spitfire and Messerschmitt, who almost grew
hooked on the glue which filmed around his fingers.

II

Word Processor

I'm tap-tapping words into this weird box.
Trowel in hand, you kneel beside flowers.

The cursor blinks its non-stop invitations –
enough to give anyone writer's block.

You, too, have paused. You straighten, smooth your hair,
your scrutiny a critic's finding fault.

Green secrets plotted against a black ground!
The times I've pestered you with "And what's that?"

Your patient answers never seem to stick.
Over my screen I watch you stoop,

bed the new plants ... Should I print out these lines,
you'd hear a noise – high-pitched but growing hoarse,

which might bring Morse code or a cry to mind –
then maybe glance towards my unlatched window.

Wedding Dress

Virginal, folded, it lies in its box,
this costly symbol you've decided to sell.

"I don't think," you tease, "I'll need it again."
The day you and your mother bought it from Harrods

your purse was stolen in the jostling Tube.
That evening, you were starry-eyed, fed up.

Soon we would swear "In sickness and in health,"
our mouths dry, voices steady ... Side by side,

we joke while a friend admires the stitching:
"No chance now of your descending the stairs

like Mary Tyrone, dress borne in your arms,
'happy for a time'!" You laugh at my play

with the glum scenario, your face tilted
towards me as when, veiled, you'd reached the altar.

Accidents

My seeing this fiery whirl involved
your hands' arrangements, plus the chance

that led me to a room where sunlight makes
roses blaze from the vase

you picked up in a shop at Albert Dock.
Those cargoes of bric-a-brac! Stilled warehouses!

We seemed to look on while a great wheel turned . . .
But why so late? Scenes stage themselves:

you in a car-smash, the knock at the door,
grave accents of the bringer of bad news.

"Trifles will outlive us," I mutter
— such as the vase which now you're bearing off:

"These flowers are parched." Out for a run,
I pass a crashed Ford and patrol lights whirling.

An Imperfect Spy

Your parents' new flat hidden off Sefton Park –
security's a worry we've discussed.

I spied le Carré's latest on the floor:
"A much-dropped name these days!" "Well, pick it up."

A mounted college oar looks down on me
while, hooked, I see how I could see myself

in this agent who dodges roles that chose him;
or did he choose them, needing the cover?

Soon simply reading feels like treachery . . .
An inquisitive sun peers through the window,

alighting on your hair as you come in.
The room yields to you, throws off suspicion

– although the sentence I transcribed still bites:
Even when you are telling the truth, you lie.

The Twinning

Evening enters the kitchen like a spirit
I had taken, unaccountably, for granted.
You are sketching heart-shaped ivy leaves; they
curl, a transplanted still life, on the table.

The sky is twilit, early, almost evil.
Switched on like artificial light, a new
moon haloes you, but blanches me
as if I'd chanced upon a virginal presence.

When the fridge falls dumb a veil seems to lift.
I glimpse a no-man's-land where lunar secrets
whisper through leaf and fingers. Before you stop,
the window catches the crook of your arm,
twinning you with a world I dare not take
for granted, even when clouds occlude the moon.

Shades of Grey

Over my head, you drift round the bedroom.
I'm glued to the late film, *Marienbad*,

compelled by what I once thought "pseud".
Beyond a vast hotel the vistas freeze.

Frames shot in black and white yield shades of grey,
this riddling couple ...

He says they met last year, had an affair.
She tests him, *Tell me the rest of our story*.

Winters ago we strolled home, arm in arm,
our verdict clear: "The man trumped up the past."

But soon, beside you, I'll dream of a maze
where shapes, our doubles, trace and retrace steps

– or so I conceive when subtitles claim:
Again I walked down these same corridors.

Parallels

I happened, the March we were sure,
to buy a copy of *Poets in their Youth*.

Film-wrapped, it promised contrasts, parallels ...
Day-dreaming in my study, weighing phrases,

I'd just thought of one for the Russian Vine
that "flowered mockingly" around our shed

when, eyes lowered back to print, I choked
on Eileen Simpson's account of Berryman

leaving out for her, his child-wanting wife,
Yerma with a note that urged "*Read!*" I did.

Not us remotely – but those cadences,
inventions of distress ...

Look how I'm left alone! As if the moon
searched for herself in the sky. Look at me.

Two Cards, Two Candles

"Two cards," you say and lift them with a smile
which is no smile. "How tasteful," I'd reply
if a joke were on ...
"A new mother; a mother

who's soon to have a hysterectomy."
The pairing defeats us; you slip inside,
blind from the glare, mind's eye on what's to come:
paying the call, unable not to hold

it as your own; ladling out sympathy
until you could ... In that Rocamadour chapel
where couples petition a shady madonna

you thought about a three-franc candle, but
wondered with a smile which was no smile whether
one costing ten would melt her heart more surely.

On the Threshold

The Moses basket – rushy, lined
(I stooped above it yesterday);

the mobile dangling in mid-air;
wallpaper asterisked by stars.

Over the months you've kitted out
my former study: "We might hear any time."

A moment back your "Have a look" ascended . . .
"The social worker will love this:

just one thing needed, a baby to adopt!"
But the snow of drafts that had missed the target

and lay round the stacked bin
– while we pause on the threshold

I'm staring hard at the hurt
my failure to find words for keeps from melting.

Upheavals

For weeks now they've been digging up the road.
Mustard-coloured gas pipes. Cordoned trenches.
"It's worse than the War!" grumbles a neighbour
– weather-beaten veteran of the terrace.

Our doors close on a drill
that jars the chill afternoon. I drop my bag,
uncurl numbed fingers, then glance at my watch.
Good. Enter the man from the Halifax

to check our loft-conversion. "My bolt-hole,"
I joke, "should our adoption plans work out."
He smiles politely. While I lead him up,

a young girl – local – maybe shivers
in a bus queue, enduring her secret.
Clouds float above skylights. She counts the months.

Naming

The phone's spondaic trill –
we hope it signals long-awaited news:
"There's a baby." Just a wrong number;
but, tempting fate, we bandy syllables,

eager as quiz contestants till I smile:
"What's in a name?" Euphony, dissonance
– the "natural mother" ("Must you?") choosing first,
the birth certificate, tag on the cot.

Last week we travelled from my parents' house
back to the North East, our adopted home.
Signs made me brood on etymologies:

Coneythorpe, Leeming, Catterick, Belmont . . .
A boy, I woke to find the dark a hive
buzzing with souls – an unborn, nameless swarm.

A Flipped Coin

To be wryly paternal was the idea,
to compose "A Prayer for my Son" ...

I haven't jotted down a syllable.
A snowy tabula rasa stares me out.

The summer night casually breezes in.
When a goods train bangs past my desk vibrates.

Tremors and rumours – earlier,
I switched a crisis-laden programme off

to catch your bulletin from the front line:
"He's kicked the quilt back, but still sleeps,

clutching his rag with a trust which brings the ..."
I pick up my pen, look towards the sky

and, for an instant, imagine the globe
as a flipped coin careering God knows where.

Maundy Thursday

Under my chair, you scatter analogues.
Duplo Babels topple and rise again . . .

"Daddy would like to read his Keats."
You crawl resignedly to where sleeved records

plead to be flexed. My anguished "Don't!"
earns me a look so injured it would make

the stoniest heart *too small to hold its blood.*
I give Moneta up, then you a hug . . .

And now you're whisked, indignant, to the bath.
Presto's my fate. Prowling aisle after aisle,

I wonder what to buy for supper, what . . .
The child I was would bare, at much this hour,

a well-scrubbed foot for the bowed priest
while candle-light washed shadows from the altar.

Clutter

I brace myself to hoist you to the attic . . .
You squeal for the Mr Happy toothbrush

that bristles in a mug along with ours.
How quickly he's become a part of us.

When we adopted you a year ago,
I'd chipped a finger playing five-a-side.

Those midnight twinges in the rocking chair.
The audible assurance of your breath . . .

Soon the healed digit, a wand wagging "No",
has conjured up the foster mother's house

where, gingerly cradling you, I wore the splint
you're all agog to reach for on my desk

whose clutter would, it strikes me rawly, be
– were you not here – the merest papering over.

III

Christmas Eve

The more than usually vulnerable –
their sufferings huddle at the pane this midnight
like moths or wan carols. I watch the light
thrown out on snow-ribbed tarmac by a candle

and think of those whose families have made
living a web spun by spidery malice,
of those lacking a stance to buttress weakness,
those a brusque word cuts open like a blade.

Their thin chorus of cries will finish soon.
I wish for them night's anaesthetized gift
of sleep, or solitude, while slow winds drift
between flame-ghosted snow and a stone moon.

Seminar

Our subject this week's "What is tragedy?",
yet seems, well ... comic. Polonius-like,
I'm stuck behind the arras of a desk.

Someone wheels in Aristotle
pat on his cue: the "tragic flaw", that key,
A-level gospel, crutch my students grasp.

"Why should a dog, a horse, a rat have life ...?"
I mouth my touchstone. But the words float free
and fall flat – balloons pricked by pointed yawns.

What scenes await these faces? Windows mist.

"... And thou no breath at all," I murmur – then
a second wind conveys us past "catharsis".

Chairs rasp. In need of air I drift outside.
Groups hover, scarved, braving perspectives.

Wheeling the Kids

We'd meant to mooch off early that last Sunday,
broach some serious talk – Rilke, God . . .

Instead, we found ourselves wheeling the kids,
imperious in their buggies, to the Parks.

"C'est la vie," as one of us must have muttered
– not that we'd have it otherwise,

or so the hewn calm of your fine profile
while you watched the tree our sons tottered round

seemed to say, your look resurrecting
the noon we nursed our coffee in the shadow

of Chartres . . . Those buttresses, towers
and north-porch patriarchs dreaming of Christ

confirmed what you had trustfully divined,
yet needled me like Rilke's "change your life".

Casting

You'd laugh or frown at the roles I've cast us in . . .
Reading *Narziss and Goldmund* as a student,

I made-believe we were those rivals, brothers:
the one destined to wander, love, create;

the other to stay put, advise, reflect.
A polarizing myth . . . yet, on a visit

from Italy with your girlfriend,
you dig out battered poems for my comments.

As always, line after line overpowers.
Infinite riches! I prod the grammar,

query the odd adjective, play the pedant . . .
In this photo snapped at a wedding

we toast each other, scene set up by me,
needing the evidence of our lasting smiles.

Beatrice and her Friend

Beatrice and her friend whose name has gone
though I've a sense of veil-dark hair

parted down the middle, of a taut mouth
that widened rarely into shadowy smiles . . .

A wooden cabin – *echt* New England – where
fazed counsellors escaped from kids

allowed the pick-me-up of talk while tracks
like "Melissa" wailed: *knowing many, loving none.*

I might still, green flares stretched out before me,
be waiting my turn to put my oar in

as when we slid across the star-chilled lake,
the wakes of three canoes moving together,

apart . . . Tonight, they're cadences, paired muses,
Beatrice and her friend whose name has gone.

Zip Code

Sending-out day. Some library in the States.
I scribble numbers on an envelope,

break off, look up. The window brings to light
the lamp's self-centred halo, my bleared face.

Beyond lie darkness, space, a postscript scrawled
like a vapour trail: *Don't you have a zip code?*

She feared those airmailed letters might get lost.

One, almost the last, I skip-read
while a clipped voice analysed "The Wanderer".

That lecture-theatre's superwatted dazzle ...
Her High School traumas swam before my eyes,

went under. Soon it would all seem a fiction,
the beach where she rode bareback make-believe,
the town my train abandoned never there.

The Last Visit

Ten miles you hiked to school across the mountains.
My flashback sparked within that tenebrous
room when you grasped my upset hand, and said
in Cork gutturals still speaking out for life,

"Patior." Always the scholar. A boy,
I'd scan the worn spines of classical texts
lining your mage-like study, while August
rewrote light's alphabet on seasoned grain.

And there my father would laugh with affection
at sepia holes drilled through your favourites,
Homer well and truly parsed by mosquitoes.

I imagine you, a missionary, reading,
fireflies irradiating foreign dusk,
your gaze firm as your mother-tongued "I suffer."

Spring Visitor

These freckling boughs. They're almost your arms wav
You've found ways of visiting me this spring.
The draining harms leukaemia did to you
– bruises like blue coins on your fine hands –

seemed fresh as ever when I saw your ring
wink from my sister's finger emerald
reminders of so much – your Irishness,
spirits waxing and drooping like a sea.

Continually, as now in this garden,
I seem to enter rooms where talk's just ended.
The *Coriolanus* you gave me flutters open

and your maiden name, inscribed with a flourish,
dances while light blesses each character.
I almost hear steps fade when evening comes.

The Other Side

Today a student riled by Beckett left
me fuming, smiling. "Why," she keened,

"does he go in for what you call 'mixed tones'?"
The imprinted image of her enraged face

might drive me up the wall, but sends me off
across my attic floor . . . Your funeral –

how low we were, yet, in the cemetery,
when the priest fished from his cassock a squirter

primed with holy water, laughter broke loose,
had to be stifled behind hankies, frowns . . .

A train stretches beyond the Velux window,
hurtled illumination that, fleeing, stays

just long enough to let me glimpse thin boughs,
their grave dance the other side of the lines.

Bible Study

I pored over the fourth Gospel,
spurred on by long-lapsed fervour.
"In the beginning was the Word ..." etc.
That my *Jerusalem Bible*

had come from you I'd forgotten.
By the time I spied your name and a date
fervour had lost its heat
– I suppose I needed a sign ...

You sent me one when I flicked to Luke.
Out slipped a press cutting, my name
jostling others – the class list of some exam.
Whatever rose again from your good book

called up a boy's eyes bidden from his page
less by the voice than the small, still smile
while tongues of fire played about a coal
they'd soon dislodge.

Revenant

Whose figure was flickering, Jon,
if not yours just now on the stair?
Courteous, edgy revenant,
you tail my footsteps everywhere.

I walk out, wrestling with your death,
that choice forced on you by despair
when all the purposes of breath
stuck in your throat: polluted air.

She ditched you. Was the killer "Why"?
Inside, my call's a played-down prayer
for you to glide from cover, shy
hand running through a maze of hair.

The Uses of Literature

You were dying, those baked summer days,
in a terminal bed,
while I was in this airy library, working hard
for a footling Shakespeare Prize

I knew I'd never win.
Q and F. Such an expense of spirit.
The clock's dull tock struck out each minute.
Then came your transcription

of Gray's "Elegy" in that last letter,
your writing almost too shaky to read ...
Finally, your hoarse riddle, hands limp on the sheet,
Don't let them get you – which I return to here.

IV

A Drive at Night

The day has driven itself to this:
headlamps interrogating, no cat's-eyes,
nerves screwing tighter as bends peer,
chevron-lidded, towards us.

I start to forget Wastwater's sheer
screes corded like twists in a giant hour
-glass. An unbraiding remembrance
while tyres grip and waver.

Silenced, breathing a petrol trance,
faculties bent on resistance,
we head like shadow selves for sleep.
Dreams will work up each glance

at charged, electric hedgerows, sheep
clattering over stiles to crop
alien dark, darkness's windstreaming
tunnels which will not stop.

Jogging

The homeward route begins to hurt.
The cathedral flaunts its upright facade

across threatened allotments, leaf-screened graves.
Thirty-five tomorrow – *nel mezzo del cammin* . . .

"If 200 minus your age is more
than twice your usual pulse rate you're okay":

the words beat, mantra-like, against my temples
before I let the swim of figures spill,

negotiate a junction, eye on a car
which might slew sideways, should its driver's heart . . .

Perhaps I'll live for ever if I run
so zealously that flesh turns into spirit

– the jogger's half-baked credo. My son, now
nineteen months, grins to see me enter, panting.

Questions of Honour

At a loss in this civilian zone
where sunlight takes its ease outside the pub,
a muscled soldier sets down his chair
closer to mine. A gravelled sound.
"What a dead town!" Reconnoitring his pint,

he homes in: "Ever read *The Flashman Papers?*"
His sacred text . . . Amazement
wounds his eyes when I shake my head.
"A tyrant, bully, yet a brave man"
– he croons the phrases like a spell.

Then, abrupt as a challenge,
"I'm a coward." The drink?
Or a small voice piping up in a mind
like a mid-Victorian dormitory
rent, after Lights Out, by questions of honour?

Trespass

The veldt sleeps under stars as white
as a pioneer who has come to stay

– the opening of my elegy for Biko,
my conscience on my sleeve and written out.

What followed I'd forgotten I'd repressed
until a whip of sunlight cracked bold type:
"Nightmare in the townships". I winced,

retraced those steps to a phone-box
where I would right a "small misunderstanding".

My lines, well-meaning, had upset your friend –
Indian, exiled from South Africa.

How much I'd trespassed hit me while we spoke.
"He . . . he was special to us." Were those tears?

The door's weight. I stood outside, shamed. Stars whitened.

Reflection

It sways behind you now, the wood of shadow
which took form between your locked car

and the path that leads to the library.
There's a moment of relief, like a clearing.

You glimpse a girl who walks away
from erudition's tiered cage of light.

She might, you catch yourself reflecting, stand
for the object of writing – how you see it

as it fades. Revolving doors receive you,
whirling your face to smithereens

before you recompose yourself and move
from bay to bay in search of lines

you've had at the back of your mind all week . . .
Here they are, bleaker than you remembered.

Hartlepool Sea Front

A plaque commemorates a killing
dealt by a German cruiser's shell.
A cannon from Sebastopol
struts, out of place as we who, strolling

past ships, cove and breakwater, watch
gulls surf in rows or ride a wind
that chafes men shovelling where sand
meets waves, where eked-out sea coal's cash.

Sunset squanders golds and yellows.
Seaweed tightens its belt-like hold.
Stiff houses, gone down in the world,
overlook our dawdling shadows.

The Pianist

His muscle-pebbled jaw
ruminates on perfection.
His skull's an echo-chamber,
vibrantly soundless.

Rigour possesses him:
an interior metronome;
a dark familiar.
It has its own music,

sponsor and rival
to that other music
fingers animate:
we hear their counterpoint;

and windfalls of bruised fruit,
pedal-ripened,
nestle in our ears,
then rot in a rich silence.

The Stripped Bed

I lie on the stripped bed
where darkness foxed a child:
Had my father just called?
Shadows loomed – Satan, God . . .

His tenor scales the pipes.
I doze off . . . Close to sleep,
I start as from a trap.
Roofs wane; night seals its lips.

Uncurtained, grown-up room!
My pulse slows while I scan
the raked lights of a plane.
Droning, programmed for home,

it shears through clouds, but hangs
in front of me an age –
frail, burdened fuselage
scarcely sustained by wings.